GUIDE TO FINANCIAL RESPONSIBILITY

Should I Go to College?

Carla Mooney

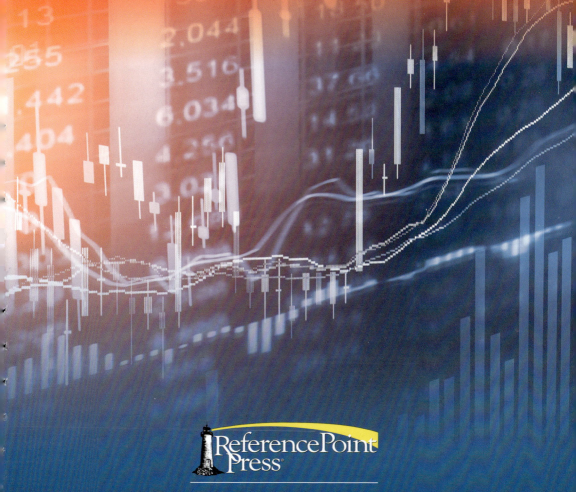

ReferencePoint Press®

San Diego, CA

About the Author

Carla Mooney is the author of many books for young adults and children. She lives in Pittsburgh, Pennsylvania, with her husband and three children.

© 2024 ReferencePoint Press, Inc.
Printed in the United States

For more information, contact:
ReferencePoint Press, Inc.
PO Box 27779
San Diego, CA 92198
www.ReferencePointPress.com

ALL RIGHTS RESERVED.
No part of this work covered by the copyright hereon may be reproduced or used in any form or by any means—graphic, electronic, or mechanical, including photocopying, recording, taping, web distribution, or information storage retrieval systems—without the written permission of the publisher.

LIBRARY OF CONGRESS CATALOGING-IN-PUBLICATION DATA

Names: Mooney, Carla, 1970- author.
Title: Should I go to college? / by Carla Mooney.
Description: San Diego, CA : ReferencePoint Press, Inc., 2023. | Series: Guide to financial responsibility | Includes bibliographical references and index.
Identifiers: LCCN 2023018838 (print) | LCCN 2023018839 (ebook) | ISBN 9781678205607 (library binding) | ISBN 9781678205614 (ebook)
Subjects: LCSH: College choice--United States--Juvenile literature. | College student orientation--United States--Juvenile literature.
Classification: LCC LB2350.5 .M66 2023 (print) | LCC LB2350.5 (ebook) | DDC 378.1/610973--dc23/eng/20230426
LC record available at https://lccn.loc.gov/2023018838
LC ebook record available at https://lccn.loc.gov/2023018839

CONTENTS

Introduction   4
An Important Decision

Chapter One   8
Is College Right for You?

Chapter Two   17
How Will You Pay for College?

Chapter Three   27
Other Education Options

Chapter Four   36
Taking a Gap Year

Chapter Five   45
Alternatives to College

Source Notes	54
Glossary	57
For More Information	58
Index	60
Picture Credits	64

INTRODUCTION

An Important Decision

Where are you going to college? It is a question that high school seniors face from friends, family, teachers, coaches, and other interested individuals. For many teens, going to college is the expected next step after high school graduation. Princesa Ceballos, a high school junior living in California's San Joaquin Valley, is excited to attend college. She is the daughter of immigrants, and her two older brothers went to college and now work as teachers. "They were both the first in our family to go to college, so they were a big inspiration," Ceballos says. Ceballos plans to become an agronomist, a soil scientist. She intends to major in environmental science with a minor in agricultural business to follow that career path. She has researched colleges and picked one she thinks is a good fit: California Polytechnic State University at San Luis Obispo. "I want to be able to get my bachelor's and my master's and eventually my doctorate degree, even though it's really expensive," Ceballos says. "Especially being a woman in, possibly, a STEM field, I think I want to be able to motivate others—once I do graduate—younger than me to pursue those types of careers."[1]

A Different Path

Though Ceballos is looking forward to higher education, college may not be the right choice for everyone. Rising college costs and student loans make many people consider alternative pathways into the workforce. Students are considering the value of career training and the availability of jobs when deciding what path to take after high school. "Students . . . are looking at education through a practical lens. They want to know what the cost is, how they're going to pay, how they will get through everyday life and whether there's a job at the end of the road,"[2] says Dan Fisher, president and chief executive officer (CEO) of the ECMC Group, a nonprofit that aims to help students succeed.

> "Students . . . are looking at education through a practical lens. They want to know what the cost is, how they're going to pay, how they will get through everyday life and whether there's a job at the end of the road."[2]
>
> —Dan Fisher, president and CEO of the ECMC Group

Vernell Cheneau III has decided that college is not right for him now. Cheneau is a high school senior from New Orleans. Although he is still in high school, Cheneau is already working hard. In addition to his schoolwork, he edits audio and video for a digital media production internship and has a thriving business reselling sneakers and phone cases on online marketplaces.

Cheneau has thought a lot about going to college, but he has decided that it is not worthwhile for him given his present career opportunities. "This is a school, an institution that I am paying money for—an investment," Cheneau says. "Do I think that the knowledge that these people will teach me is going to be worth it in the end? I did the calculations to myself. Wasn't worth it in the end."[3]

Instead of heading to college after high school graduation, Cheneau has already landed a job. He will work in the human resources department of Entergy, a Fortune 500 energy company. Cheneau landed the job after participating in a high school workforce fellowship, which enabled him to earn certifications in email marketing, inbound sales, and Autodesk Inventor design software. He is excited to make good money at Entergy and to be one of the few people the company has hired right out of high school. "That's big, especially for me, you know, knowing what I

For many teens, going to college is the given next step after high school graduation. But it may not be the right choice for everyone.

can do with that money and that experience and those connections," he says. "Things of that nature are just invaluable."[4]

Long term, Cheneau wants to become an entrepreneur and own a business. His family has encouraged him to work toward becoming his own boss. "Don't be a chef—own a restaurant. Don't be a doctor—own a hospital. So now, I have that 'I have to have my own' mentality,"[5] he says.

Choosing a Path

Going to college is one of the first significant decisions teens will make. Students who choose to attend college are investing considerable time and money to further their education. For many students, college can be a stepping stone to landing a well-paying job and building a career that interests and engages them.

Although many students choose to pursue education, more are choosing alternative paths. According to data from the National Student Clearinghouse, undergraduate enrollment nationwide has dropped 8 percent from 2019 to 2022. It is the steepest decline in college enrollment on record, according to the US Bureau of Labor Statistics. Education officials say that student debt concerns and better access to jobs without a college degree have made college less attractive to students. "This generation is different. They're more pragmatic about the way they work, about the way they spend their time and their money,"[6] says Jamia Stokes, a senior director at SCORE, an educational nonprofit. Most young people are simply more aware of the opportunities and the costs—and have more tools to weigh them—so that they can make more-informed decisions about their future.

CHAPTER ONE

Is College Right for You?

Are you wondering if college is right for you? The decision of whether to go to college is a big one, and earning a college degree is a significant investment, both in time and money. You might be wondering if college is worth it. And there is no right or wrong answer to this question. Sometimes, college may be the right choice, but other times, an alternate path may be better. The answer depends on each person's circumstances and future goals.

The Benefits of College

Millions of people attend colleges nationwide. Earning a college degree can have financial, professional, and personal benefits. Most students believe earning a college degree will open the door to better job opportunities and higher incomes. Studies prove them right. People with a bachelor's degree earn about $36,000 more annually, or 84 percent higher, than people whose highest degree is a high school diploma, according to the Association of Public and Land Grant Universities. Over a lifetime, that earnings gap adds up, with college graduates earning an average of $1.2 million more than those with a high school diploma.

Also, research shows people with a college degree are more likely to be employed. According to Bureau of Labor Statistics data, unemployment rates typically decline as educational levels rise. For example, in February 2023, people who did not finish high school had an unemployment rate of 5.8 percent, whereas people with a bachelor's degree had an unemployment rate of 2.0 percent.

Going to college can also help you connect with other students and professors who may help you professionally. Many colleges have career offices that help graduates land jobs and network with employers and alumni. "Alumni networks . . . are powerful and willing communities that can create jobs and internships and increase the marketplace value of their institutions' degrees,"[7] says Andrew Margie, cofounder and CEO of Alumnifire.

What Are Your Career Goals?

So how do you decide if college is right for you? Knowing what work you want to do, especially when you are still in high school, can be difficult. Take some time to assess your interests and skills. Some schools have questionnaires that help students identify potential careers that match their interests. Once you have chosen a possible career that interests you, research the requirements to work in that field. Do you need to go to college to work in that career, or does another educational path make more sense?

For some careers, college is a must. Doctors, lawyers, accountants, and engineers are just some professions for which a bachelor's degree or higher is necessary. Jobs involving research, scientific, or professional work usually require candidates to have at least a bachelor's degree in a specific study area. For these careers, college makes sense because students learn skills and knowledge that they will use daily on the job.

For Victoria Meuse, a bachelor's degree led to a job. She earned a bachelor's degree in psychology, which helped her get a job as a teacher at her children's elementary school. "Right now, I love working at my kids' school. I think that the background in psychology has helped me a lot in understanding the students,"[8] says Meuse.

For some jobs, employers will not look at potential employees who do not have a college degree. Some want job applicants to have a degree in a specific field, but others are flexible with the area of study. Therefore, if the type of job you want typically only hires people with a bachelor's degree, college may be the right choice for you.

But not every job or career requires a four-year college degree. And there are several well-paying, in-demand jobs you do not have to go to college to get. According to the Georgetown University Center on Education and the Workforce, in the United States, about 30 million jobs pay an average of $55,000 annually that do not require a bachelor's degree. Are you interested in becoming a chef, plumber, electrician, or pilot? These are just a few good careers for which you do not need a college degree. For these careers, the necessary skills may be best learned at a technical school or on the job. "The good news is that there are plenty of occupations out

According to recent studies, graduates with a bachelor's degree earn about $36,000 more annually than people whose highest degree is a high school diploma.

there that pay well without a college degree,"[9] says Ryan Farrell, an economist at the Bureau of Labor Statistics. For people interested in careers in these areas, college may not be the right path.

> "The good news is that there are plenty of occupations out there that pay well without a college degree."[9]
>
> —Ryan Farrell, an economist at the Bureau of Labor Statistics

When Garret Morgan was in high school, many people told him to go to college and get a bachelor's degree. "All through my life it was, 'If you don't go to college you're going to end up on the streets.' Everybody's so gung-ho about going to college," he says. Morgan initially tried college but eventually decided it was not for him. He quit college and began training as an ironworker. Five years later, he is working full-time and helping to build the Rainier Square Tower in Seattle and a data center for Microsoft. "I'm loving it every day. It was absolutely the right choice,"[10] he says. And he jokes that someday his high school friends who went to college will earn as much as he earns now.

Still not sure about the career you want? You are not alone. Many teens go to college planning one path and end up switching majors and pursuing another field. For many people, college can offer exposure to many subjects not offered at their high school and thus didn't know they would like. However, switching majors until you find the right fit can make the path to graduation longer and more expensive. If you have the money and time, that is not a problem, but for others with a tighter budget, it may be beneficial to put off college until they are more focused on what they want to study. "College is the biggest training system for careers in the country and a college credential is your ticket into a career. Having said all of that, it's really important that you have an idea of what you want to do. Finding your way through college and taking seven or eight years to get a bachelor's degree—most of us don't have the time or the money to do that anymore,"[11] says Martin Van Der Werf, associate director of editorial and postsecondary policy at the Georgetown University Center on Education and the Workforce.

College Graduates: Healthy and Happy

College graduates may live healthier lives. Studies have shown a link between more education and better health. People whose highest educational level is a high school diploma are nearly twice as likely to report poorer health than those who have completed a college degree. One 2021 study by researchers at the College of William and Mary in Virginia found that college graduates had healthier lifestyles, including getting adequate physical exercise, maintaining healthy body weight, and refraining from smoking. College graduates also enjoyed higher earnings and better working conditions, contributing to overall health. Research also suggests that college graduates lead happier lives. Several surveys show people with a high school diploma are less likely to report being satisfied with their lives than are college graduates. "Education is probably more strongly correlated with future happiness throughout adulthood than any other variable," says Jeffrey Arnett, a developmental psychologist and professor of psychology at Clark University in Worcester, Massachusetts.

Quoted in Cory Stieg, "From the Best Major to Finding Purpose in Life—How Going to College Affects Your Happiness," CNBC, August 17, 2020. www.cnbc.com.

Consider the Finances

College is expensive. For the 2021–2022 school year, the average private college cost more than $38,000 annually, according to *U.S. News & World Report*. Public state colleges are less expensive but cost nearly $23,000 for out-of-state students and more than $10,000 for in-state students. And that is just tuition costs. Most college students must pay thousands more yearly for room and board, fees, books, and other school expenses. Multiply those costs over four years, and you will see how quickly the costs of college add up.

However, many schools offer students financial help through grants, scholarships, and loans. Grant and scholarship programs can reduce the cost of college and make it more affordable for students. Student loans from the federal government and private lenders are also available and can help finance a college degree.

Although most students receive some financial aid, often it is not enough to cover all college costs. As a result, they frequently take out student loans to finance their education. Student debt can quickly balloon out of control if not managed properly. Many college graduates find their student debt burdens them for years.

When deciding if college is right for you, you must consider your finances. Determine the cost for the schools that you might attend. Remember that in many cases, an in-state public college will be less expensive than a private college. How much money do you or your family have saved to pay for college? And how much financial aid do you expect to receive?

Once you have looked at these numbers, you will know how much money you can expect to pay each year for college. Some people can pay their college bills from savings or out of their current income. Others, however, do not have the means, so they take out private student loans to finance their education. You might want to rethink your plans if you need to take out large loans to afford college. Instead of putting yourself into significant debt, you might try alternative educational paths, such as starting at a less expensive community college or working to earn and save money for college. "Your earnings now can be used later, if you decide to continue advancing your education,"[12] says Mack Smith, a college instructor who has helped develop educational programs and counseled students about their career paths.

There are about 30 million jobs that pay an average of $55,000 annually that do not require a bachelor's degree. A chef is one example of a career for which you do not need a college degree.

Life Circumstances

An individual's life circumstances can also be a factor in college plans. Enrolling in college is a big commitment in time, and students often must put other interests on hold while focusing on their education. However, some responsibilities cannot be put on hold. For example, people who are the primary caregivers for a family member or child may be unable to devote the time and money required to earn a college degree.

Tysa Rose is a single mother in Fargo, North Dakota, and she understands the struggle of balancing her responsibilities as a mother and as a college student. She initially enrolled in her local community college and selected classes that allowed her to keep working full time to afford rent and day care for her daughter. Despite her efforts, she struggled once classes started. The inexpensive laptop she purchased could not run some of the software programs she needed for school, and she did not pass those courses. Also, because Rose's daughter has some medical needs that require weekly physical and occupational therapy, Rose's

Enrolling in college is a big commitment in time. People who are primary caregivers for someone may be unable to devote the time and money required to earn a degree.

Are You Academically Prepared?

For college to have the greatest return on investment, students need to earn a degree. Students who do not finish college still have student loan debt, but they lack the degree that could help them land a better job. According to a 2022 report by the Education Data Initiative, nearly 33 percent of college students will not complete their degree program. Many will drop out of school because they are not academically prepared to handle college. If students struggle academically in high school, they might want to consider starting at a community college. In these programs, students can take the time to build their academic skills and determine the right career path. Many community colleges have agreements with four-year universities that the credits students earn at the community college can transfer to the university's degree program. This can help individuals get accustomed to higher education and move through classes at their own pace.

schedule of work, school, day care, and medical appointments quickly became overwhelming. Rose decided to put her college plans on hold. "I decided, 'Maybe just focus on trying to make sure you keep your job because that's paying your rent, that's paying your daughter's daycare,'"[13] she says.

However, the rise of remote learning and online college programs has made it possible for more people to attend college. These technologies make earning a college degree easier for people with livelihoods that prevent them from attending traditional in-person classes. For Samantha Campbell of Jacksonville, Florida, online courses allowed her to earn a college degree. When she was laid off, Campbell's husband suggested she go to college and earn a degree. But at the time, Campbell had young children at home, and the child care she would need to attend in-person classes was not affordable. Instead, she turned to online courses and enrolled in Florida State College at Jacksonville to earn a bachelor's degree in education. "Online college has helped me tremendously. I have six children, and childcare costs are astronomical. Since I take most of my classes online, I can avoid the cost associated with childcare and gas. I can still obtain my education and still be in a position to take care of my family responsibilities,"[14] she says.

Develop Marketable Skills

Whether you go to college or pursue an alternative educational path, developing marketable skills should be a top priority. Having the skills employers desire will help you build a successful career. "Whether you want to work for yourself or get a good job working for someone else, what you really need are in-demand skills. Think about the most cost-efficient way to develop the skills you need in a career that you will find fulfilling,"[15] says Smith.

> "Whether you want to work for yourself or get a good job working for someone else, what you really need are in-demand skills. Think about the most cost-efficient way to develop the skills you need in a career that you will find fulfilling."[15]
>
> —Mack Smith, a college instructor

For some, a traditional four-year college degree and possibly advanced degrees may be the best way to build those skills. Students who are ready for the academic challenges of college, have the time and money, and are in a career field where they expect to get a reasonable return on their investment may find choosing college is the right decision.

For others, however, college may not be the best way to learn the necessary skills. Sometimes, alternative educational paths can be a better way to learn the skills you need for long-term career success. "Be honest about what you want and where you're at," suggests Smith. "There are plenty of career programs and technical education programs that can help you accomplish your goals. Don't get hung up on going to college once you realize that it's not actually for you."[16]

Whatever high school students decide, they always have the flexibility to change their minds. Some students decide they are not ready for college right out of high school and instead work for a few years. Later, they decide they want to go to college after all. In many cases, they can and are successful in doing so.

CHAPTER TWO

How Will You Pay for College?

When deciding if college is right for you, it is essential to think realistically about costs. Depending on your chosen college, the cost of tuition and room and board can vary by tens of thousands of dollars. Some of the most expensive colleges are excellent schools, but there are many less costly colleges that provide good educations. There are also ways for students to get help paying for college, no matter which college they choose.

The High Cost of College

College is expensive. According to *U.S. News & World Report*, the average annual tuition for public, four-year colleges was more than $10,000 for in-state students and nearly $23,000 for out-of-state students for the 2021–2022 school year. The average annual tuition costs for private colleges were even higher at $38,000. And tuition is just part of the cost of college. Room and board, books, and other fees can add another $10,000 to $15,000 to the bill. The costs add up quickly, and some universities cost students more than $70,000 annually.

The good news is that many students do not pay the total price for college. Instead, students and their families usually pay the amount determined after need-based financial aid and merit scholarships are applied. If grants and scholarships do not fully cover college costs, students and their families can take out federal and private loans to pay for college.

Grants and Scholarships

Grants and scholarships are financial aid for students that do not need to be paid back and can come from various sources. Some grants and scholarships are based on need, determined by calculating a student's ability to pay for college. Other grants and scholarships are based on merit, given to a student for a specific talent, academic achievement, or athletic ability.

Students receive billions of dollars in federal grants to pay for college every year. One well-known federal grant is the Pell Grant. For the 2022–2023 school year, the maximum Pell Grant was $6,895. A student's eligibility for a Pell Grant is based on need as determined by the expected family contribution, which is calculated on the Free Application for Federal Student Aid (FAFSA), a form all students must complete to apply for federal financial aid for college.

Students may also be eligible for grants and scholarships from states. To qualify for state grants and scholarships, one typically must be a state resident and attend an in-state school. The grant amount varies by state, and many states are working to increase their college grant programs.

Many universities and colleges also offer grants and scholarships to students. Some of these grants and scholarships are based on need, but others are based on merit. Several websites "have an admissions calculator that shows you your chance of being admitted to a college. It is a good way to see how you rank compared to other students. If you rank highly and apply to that college, the college itself may offer you a scholarship to attend,"[17] says Kim Stezala, a college scholarship adviser. Although college grants and scholarships do not need to be repaid, students may need to maintain specific academic or athletic standards to continue receiving that aid.

> "If you rank highly and apply to that college, the college itself may offer you a scholarship to attend."[17]
>
> —Kim Stezala, a college scholarship adviser

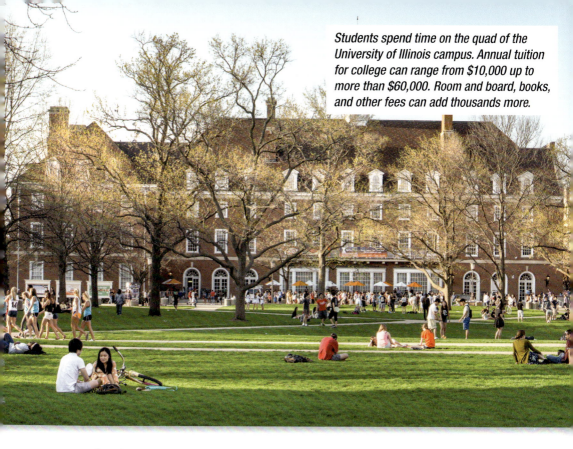

Students spend time on the quad of the University of Illinois campus. Annual tuition for college can range from $10,000 up to more than $60,000. Room and board, books, and other fees can add thousands more.

Students can also apply for grants and scholarships from corporations, private foundations, and other organizations. Often, school counselors can help find grants and scholarships for which a prospective student is eligible. "I recommend students start in their own community, school or family to really get to know themselves, their family history, memberships, involvement and employment so that they have the facts about possible scholarship connections,"[18] says Stezala.

Paying for College with Scholarships

Samantha Leach is a junior at Clemson University in South Carolina. She has managed to pay for her college tuition through scholarships and grants. While in high school, Leach began thinking about how she would pay for college. She recognized that it would be difficult for her family to foot the bill because her father had passed away years earlier, and she would have to rely on her mother and grandparents.

> "I was selected for about ten scholarships, which together were enough to pay for my entire undergrad education. Having all of college paid for is comforting."[19]
>
> —Samantha Leach, college student

As a high school senior, Leach researched college grants and scholarships and began applying. "I applied to about 60 scholarships. It took about as much work as taking an extra class. But the payoff was much more than just an A grade. I was selected for about ten scholarships, which together were enough to pay for my entire undergrad education. Having all of college paid for is comforting,"[19] she says.

Leach has some tips for students looking for help to pay for college. First, she tells students to apply for every scholarship they can. "I applied to anything I qualified for. I did the big national scholarships that are well-known; local and state scholarships; and regional scholarships, including funds for coastal communities,"[20] she says. Even though Leach thought some of the scholarships she applied for were long shots, she was pleasantly surprised to be awarded $5,000 from one of them.

Students can apply for grants and scholarships from corporations, private foundations, and other organizations. Often, school counselors can help you find those for which you are eligible.

Free Application for Federal Student Aid

The first step in applying for financial aid is filling out the Free Application for Federal Student Aid (FAFSA) on the US Department of Education website (www.ed.gov). Many schools and government agencies use the FAFSA to determine a student's financial need. The FAFSA is available starting October 1 for the following school year, and financial aid experts recommend that students and their families file their FAFSA as soon as possible. Some financial aid is awarded on a first-come, first-served basis or from a program with limited funds. Therefore, the earlier you complete the form, the better your chances of getting aid.

Being organized is essential, says Leach. She treated her applications like another class and dedicated time to them. She made a master list of every scholarship she planned to apply to, deadlines, and application requirements. She created a timeline and deadlines for herself to complete applications, just like when turning in class assignments.

According to Leach, students should prepare themselves for rejection and be able to handle it. "It's important not to get discouraged if you're not selected. There's going to be rejection involved in this process. If I didn't hear back from a scholarship, I crossed it off my list and moved on. Instead of lingering on rejection, I focused on what I could control, like applying for more scholarships,"[21] she says.

Student Loans

In many cases, grants and scholarships plus savings and income do not cover the total cost of college. To pay the remaining amount, students can take out student loans. There are different types of student loans, each with benefits and drawbacks.

Federal student loans are low-interest, fixed-rate loans from the federal government. Federal student loans are often the most affordable way to borrow for college because they typically carry lower interest rates than other loans. There are limits to how much can be borrowed, however. In the first and second years of college, dependent students (whose need is determined by reviewing their income and parents' earnings) can borrow up to $5,500. The maximum amount rises to $7,500 in the third and fourth college years, with a cumulative total loan not to be more than $31,000. Independent and graduate students have higher borrowing limits.

One of the benefits of federal student loans is that they offer flexible repayment plans. Students can choose repayment plans based on their income or even pause repayments if they have a hardship in the future. Borrowers who work in specific public service jobs may even be eligible to have their student debt forgiven. Some repayment plans let borrowers make smaller payments over an extended period. As with any loan, however, stretching out repayment will cost borrowers more interest charges.

If students need additional money to pay for college, they may qualify for state loans or loans from their colleges. Families may also take out loans, such as the federal Direct PLUS Loan. Direct PLUS Loans, available to parents with qualifying credit, have higher interest rates than federal direct student loans, making them less attractive.

Some students and families take out private loans to pay for college. Private loans often carry significantly higher interest rates and less flexible repayment plans than federal student loans, so you should shop for the best terms and rates. Because many students do not have a credit history, private lenders often require a cosigner, such as a parent, who will be responsible for paying off the loan if the student defaults on the loan.

Financial aid experts recommend that students think seriously about how much they need in private loans to pay for college. Needing private loans may indicate that the student is borrowing too much to pay for college. Experts recommend that total student debt not exceed a student's anticipated salary after graduation. For example, if you expect to earn $40,000 annually after graduation, your total student debt should not be greater than that amount to make your debt repayment manageable. Instead of borrowing significant amounts of money, students may want to consider attending a less expensive college, such as a community college.

Nearly 70 percent of all college students work while enrolled. Students work part time to earn money for personal expenses and college costs, and they also gain valuable work experience.

Working Through School

For some students, working while going to college can help reduce the burden of college costs. Nearly 70 percent of all college students work while enrolled, according to the Georgetown University Center on Education and the Workforce. Students who work part time earn money for personal expenses and college costs, and they also gain valuable work experience that can be beneficial in the future. "In typical circumstances for the average student, it's great for them to hold down a part-time job. Students who work a moderate amount of hours—up to 15, maybe 20 hours a week—those students actually on average do better in school than students who don't work at all,"[22] says Shannon Vasconcelos, director of college finance at Bright Horizons College Coach.

However, students considering working while attending school should realistically consider possible drawbacks. The

> "Students who work a moderate amount of hours—up to 15, maybe 20 hours a week—those students actually on average do better in school than students who don't work at all."[22]
>
> —Shannon Vasconcelos, director of college finance at Bright Horizons College Coach

wages they earn at on-campus jobs rarely pay enough to cover college costs in full. And if a student spends too many hours at work, academic performance may suffer. Students with significant outside responsibilities, such as playing a sport or caregiving for a family member, may find it challenging to balance work on top of their personal responsibilities.

Students should also consider the impact of earnings from a part-time job on their financial aid. Students who earn over $7,000 will lose $0.50 in financial aid for every dollar earned over the $7,000 threshold.

Tuition Assistance

Some employers offer tuition assistance programs for employees. These programs help companies attract and retain workers and give students a way to pay for college and advance their long-term career prospects. Since 2021, companies such as Walmart, Amazon, Target, Macy's, and Lowe's have offered to pay for college for millions of their US employees. For employers, tuition assistance programs are an attractive recruiting and retention tool and help train employees for management positions. "If someone can get a bachelor's degree for no cost, that is likely to increase their loyalty to their employer,"[23] says Lydia Jilek, senior director of a business management consulting company. These programs give employees a way to get a college degree without incurring significant debt.

Tuition assistance programs are not new. For years, companies have been paying for salaried employees to earn advanced degrees, such as a master's in business administration. Often, workers had to pay for tuition up front and then get reimbursed by their employers. Now, many companies have expanded tuition assistance benefits to more employees—including hourly workers, drivers, cashiers, and more—and offer to pay up to 100 percent of employees' college costs up front. Some companies offer online college programs and stipends that students can use to pay for in-person classes at local colleges.

Income Share Agreements

A unique way to pay for college is an income share agreement (ISA). An ISA is a type of student loan in which students agree to pay a fixed percentage of their income after graduation for a defined period. Specific colleges run ISA agreements for their students; however, a few private lenders also offer them. Students start making payments on an ISA after they leave school and meet an income threshold. If they lose their job, the student can postpone making payments. How much they pay each month will depend on the ISA's terms. Many ISAs have income shares between 2 percent and 10 percent. A payment cap sets the maximum amount students have to repay under their ISAs, often two times the amount borrowed. The repayment terms for ISAs usually run from two to ten years, depending on the individual agreement.

Tens of thousands of people are taking advantage of these tuition benefits through their employers. Starbucks reports that 22,000 workers were enrolled in its online college program through Arizona State University in 2022. And Guild Education, which manages such programs for several companies, including Walmart, Hilton, and Disney, reports that it worked with 130,000 students in 2022.

At Walmart, employees can choose from sixty programs focusing on skills that align with careers at the retailer. Since its inception, more than fifteen thousand employees have graduated via Walmart's college program, with thousands more currently participating. Twenty-seven-year-old Tanner Humphreys took part in Walmart's college program, earning a bachelor's degree in computer science in 2022. He started working at Walmart in 2016 in an hourly job and attempted to balance work with in-person classes at Idaho State University. But when Walmart launched its online college program in 2018, Humphreys transferred his college credits to one of the program's partner schools, Southern New Hampshire University (SNHU), to finish his degree. Now, he works as part of a cybersecurity team at Walmart headquarters.

Fast food corporation Chipotle announced in 2019 a new tuition assistance program that would fully fund college degrees. The company pays tuition for more than seventy-five online programs in business and technology at nine institutions, including Purdue University Global, Wilmington University, and Oregon State University. In these programs, students can earn associate's and bachelor's degrees. Eligible employees must have been employed with the company for at least 120 days and work at least fifteen hours per week.

Chipotle employee Daniella Malave took advantage of her employer's tuition assistance program. While working full time, she finished two years at community college with annual stipends of $5,250 from Chipotle. Then she enrolled in Chipotle's free online college program. In 2020, she earned a bachelor's degree in business management from Wilmington University. Today, twenty-four-year-old Malave works as a recruiting analyst for Chipotle. "I didn't have to pay for my education. Every time I say it out loud, I'm like, 'Is this real?'"[24] she says.

The opportunity to earn a college degree can change lives. Angela Batista was sixteen years old and homeless when she got a job at a Starbucks in New York. "College was never in my dream. I didn't even have the audacity to fantasize about it,"[25] she says. Now thirty-seven years old, Batista graduated from Arizona State University with a degree in organizational leadership in December 2022, paid for by Starbucks. And her son, also a Starbucks employee, has started classes to earn his college degree.

Factor In Finances

Finances are a factor when deciding whether to enroll in college. Although a college degree can lead to higher income and better job opportunities, students must ensure they can finance a college education without overburdening their future with student loan debt.

CHAPTER THREE

Other Education Options

A traditional four-year college degree is not the only way to get the education and skills needed for a successful career. Associate's degrees, online colleges, and vocational certificates are alternate educational paths that can lead to rewarding careers.

Earn an Associate's Degree

Many well-paying, in-demand careers only require a worker to hold a two-year degree called an associate's degree. Students in these degree programs typically take the same types of classes and learn similar information as four-year college students during their first two years. Although these programs are not as long and intense as four-year degree programs, students gain versatile, transferable skills.

A two-year degree program can be an excellent option for students for various reasons. Sometimes, the program provides the proper education and training for the students' chosen fields. Other times, students who do not know what they want to study may choose to enroll in a two-year degree program and take the time to explore different classes and figure out their future paths. Sometimes, students enroll in these programs to improve their grades before applying to a four-year college. And because two-year colleges are generally less expensive than four-year colleges, students can earn an associate's degree, pay less in tuition for two years, and then transfer to a four-year college to finish their bachelor's degree.

Some traditional universities offer associate's degrees; they are also common to community colleges, junior colleges, and some technical schools. To earn an associate's degree, students take general education classes as well as courses in their chosen field over two years. Potential fields include business administration, science, nursing, criminal justice, accounting, engineering technology, and paralegal studies. Many schools offer online classes for students wanting to balance classes with work or other responsibilities.

One of the primary advantages of an associate's degree is that it takes less time and is less expensive than a four-year bachelor's degree. And once they earn an associate's degree, students can pursue additional education if they want. Many community colleges and other schools that offer two-year degree programs expect students to transfer to a four-year college for a bachelor's

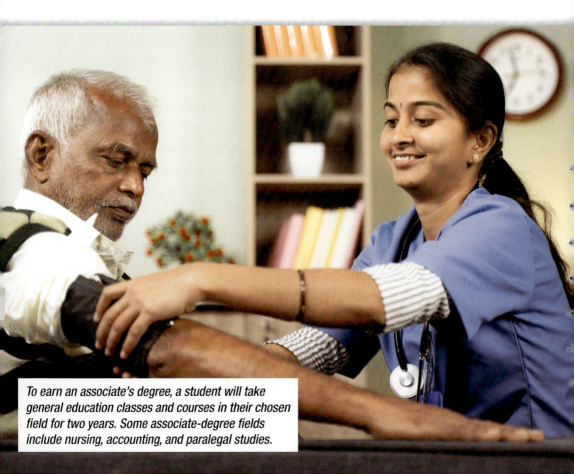

To earn an associate's degree, a student will take general education classes and courses in their chosen field for two years. Some associate-degree fields include nursing, accounting, and paralegal studies.

Types of Associate's Degrees

Associate's degrees typically come in four forms: an associate of arts (AA), an associate of science (AS), an associate of applied arts (AAA) and an associate of applied science (AAS). An AA focuses on humanities, whereas an AS involves training in STEM fields such as dentistry and information technology. Both degrees are designed to transfer to a bachelor's program at a four-year college. The AAA and AAS involve more vocational education as students explore technical subjects, such as occupational therapy and surgical technology, to prepare for jobs after graduation. All associate's degrees prepare students for the skills they will need on the job, according to Ken McQueen, a Houston-based recruiter. "Usually, associate degrees are designed to provide employees with the tools of their trade. There is less focus and attention given to social studies and other classes that are a requirement for a four-year degree. With this micro focus, on-the-job training is usually provided. Students are able to graduate and walk directly into a work environment using the same equipment used at their new jobs."

Quoted in Sammy Allen, "How Employers View an Associate Degree," *U.S. News & World Report*, October 27, 2022. www.usnews.com.

degree. Many have agreements with four-year colleges so that students can seamlessly transfer credit for work completed.

Krista Caruso is a licensed respiratory care practitioner and works at the Loma Linda University Medical Center in Loma Linda, California. When she was nineteen, she enrolled in a two-year respiratory therapy program at Victor Valley College. Although Caruso had no hospital work experience, the Victor Valley program prepared her well for her career, as she explains:

> The experience that I gained in the classroom prepared me for my clinical rotations in the hospital. Everything I learned and the situations I faced helped prepare me for my licensing exams and my transition from being a student into a Respiratory Care Practitioner. . . . The experience that I gained at Victor Valley College is priceless because it gave me the groundwork that I needed in order to build my knowledge and professional experience.[26]

Go Online for College

Advances in computer technology have opened a new path to education: online college. Instead of students taking traditional in-person classes to earn a two-year or four-year college degree, more institutions are offering a fully online option for students. These programs are more flexible, less expensive, and make maintaining a healthy school-life balance easier. While attending online college, students can keep working, care for family members, or meet other responsibilities that prevent them from attending in-person college. With online college, they can access their education anywhere at any time.

Most students at national online universities, such as SNHU and Western Governors University, are working adults looking to advance their careers through further education. However, a 2022 national survey indicates that more high school juniors and seniors plan to attend fully online colleges. "Conventional thinking says it's mostly nontraditional adult learners who utilize online [college]. Historically that has been largely true for us," says Scott Pulsipher, the president of Western Governors. "But over the past five years, the 18- to 24-year-old population has been one of our fastest-growing age categories.... We anticipate much of that demand to continue."[27] At Western Governors, the number of students ages eighteen to twenty-four enrolled has more than doubled from about six thousand students in 2017 to fifteen thousand students in 2022. As more daily activities are now commonly being done online people have become more accepting of going to college online too. "Online college isn't a leap. They think, 'I do everything else online. I'll do this online,'"[28] says Paul LeBlanc, SNHU president.

Christina Barlas originally had no plans to go to college after high school. Living outside Baltimore, she graduated from high

> "Conventional thinking says it's mostly nontraditional adult learners who utilize online [college]. ... But over the past five years, the 18- to 24-year-old population has been one of our fastest-growing age categories."[27]
>
> —Scott Pulsipher, the president of Western Governors, an online university

Traditionally, most students at online universities are working adults looking to further their education to advance in their jobs. Today, however, more high school students are planning to attend fully online colleges.

school with a cosmetology license and started work in a beauty salon. After working for a year, she decided to change careers—becoming an administrative assistant—and thought about going to college. At first, she considered in-person classes at her local community college. But the class times and commute did not fit her work schedule. Then she learned about an affordable, entirely online accelerated program at the University of Maryland's Global Campus. Barlas enrolled in 2021 and continued at her job while studying online to earn a bachelor's degree in digital media and web technology. "I personally think online is so much better. I used knowledge that I gained from classes right in the workplace,"[29] she says.

> "I personally think online [higher education] is so much better. I used knowledge that I gained from classes right in the workplace."[29]
>
> —Christina Barlas, an online college student

Vocational Programs

Some students enter vocational programs provided by technical schools, vocational colleges, and trade schools. Vocational programs offer intensive, focused training to prepare students to work in a specific job or trade. Students develop the skills they need to work in careers such as carpentry, appliance repair, automotive maintenance, real estate, medical coding, dental assisting, plumbing, cosmetology, or the culinary arts. Upon completion of the programs, students are awarded vocational certificates. Many high schools also offer technical classes, which can sometimes be applied toward a vocational certificate program.

Vocational programs are less expensive and shorter than earning a traditional four-year degree. Some certificates can take as long as two years, but students can complete many others in mere months. If students have previous experience, they may be able to complete the program earlier. As a result, vocational

Next Level Jobs

In Indiana, an initiative called Next Level Jobs provides state residents with free training for the skills needed for jobs in growing industries. The program, which began in 2017, offers tuition-free certificates in five high-demand fields: health and life sciences, information technology and business services, building and construction, transportation and logistics, and advanced manufacturing. The program supports the state's goal of having at least 60 percent of Indiana residents with an educational credential beyond a high school diploma by 2025, which will help fill projected labor needs. "We are focused on driving economic growth in Indiana and that starts with leveraging the tools we have available, beginning with education and training," Indiana governor Eric Holcomb says about the program. Holcomb praised the more than ten thousand Indiana residents who have earned certificates through the program. "Indiana is moving in the right direction and these 10,000-plus Hoosier adults that have put themselves on a better path are helping us get closer to our goal. But we're not done yet and we won't rest until all Hoosiers are skilled-up and prospering."

Quoted in "10,000 Hoosiers Complete Next Level Jobs Certificate Programs," WNDU, January 16, 2020. www.wndu.com.

students enter the workforce faster than traditional four-year college graduates. The shorter time to complete his education was a big factor for Luis Garcia when he chose to enroll at the YTI Career Institute in Pennsylvania. Instead of four years to earn a college degree, Garcia could earn the necessary certifications to become a pastry chef in two years. "A lot of companies are looking for the certifications. So this actually is helping me obtain that in a faster manner than I would if I would have to go to a four-year college,"[30] he says.

> "A lot of companies are looking for the certifications. So this actually is helping me obtain that in a faster manner than I would if I would have to go to a four-year college."[30]
>
> —Luis Garcia, a vocational student

Vocational programs are also significantly less expensive than four-year degrees. According to *Forbes*, the average total cost of a vocational certificate was $33,000 in 2022. According to the College Board, a four-year degree can cost between $109,000 to $223,000, depending on the school. Vocational programs offer significant savings, allowing students to reduce or avoid student loan debt. Also, vocational school students may be eligible for federal financial aid, scholarships, and grants.

After high school, José Santos from North Philadelphia enrolled in Williamson College of the Trades in Pennsylvania. He is studying carpentry and plans to start his own business fixing up and reselling houses after graduation. "My friends all applied to four-year colleges, and now they're in debt, and I'm not,"[31] says Santos.

Certificates and Short Courses

Some well-paying, in-demand jobs only require a certificate to get hired, and workers no longer need a four-year degree to have a satisfying career in these fields. Careers that only require a certificate are often based on skills, and employers will consider all applicants who can demonstrate the desired skills. Certificate programs are often a good option for people looking to switch careers because they are shorter, more affordable, and offer hands-on training.

Students earn certificates after completing training programs that are specialized for specific jobs or skills. Certificate programs are often offered online, allowing students to attend and study from anywhere. Earning a certificate is usually significantly faster than earning a degree. Certificate programs focus narrowly on teaching specific technical skills whereas college degree programs offer a broader education. Depending on the program, training for a certificate can last from a few months to two years. Some short certificate programs can prepare students for jobs as emergency medical technicians, personal trainers, medical coders, real estate agents, and elevator mechanics.

Some free online certificate training programs even focus on in-demand skills and prepare students with hands-on training for jobs in the tech industry. Even students who have graduated from vocational programs or colleges can add to their education by earning certificates in fields related to their careers.

Depending on the program, training for a certificate can last from a few months to two years. Some shorter certificate programs can prepare students for jobs such as a certified personal trainer.

A web developer is one example of a well-paying job you can land only with a certificate. In today's online world, businesses and organizations need websites, and they typically hire someone to create and maintain them. According to the Bureau of Labor Statistics, the demand for web developers is increasing faster than for all other occupations. Web developers create and maintain websites. They design the site's look, manage its performance, and handle troubleshooting. In a web developer certificate program, students learn the creative and technical skills for web development. They learn HTML and coding languages like Python and JavaScript. They learn to structure web pages, create responsive websites, debug programs, and more. Once they have earned the certificate, students can work as freelance web developers or land entry-level jobs within a company.

Sean Van Loggerenberg, a twenty-eight-year-old bartender from Cape Town, South Africa, enrolled in a certificate program to learn the skills needed to become a web developer. "I found programming very interesting and decided to look into it; and then I fell in love with it. The course helped a lot to build my knowledge and skills to achieve my new career goal of being a web developer. The part I enjoyed the most was interacting with other students, all of us helping each other with coding issues and solving them together,"[32] he says.

For some students, the traditional in-person college experience and four-year bachelor's degree are not the right fit. These students can succeed in alternate educational paths such as two-year degree programs, online college, vocational schools, and certificate programs.

CHAPTER FOUR

Taking a Gap Year

Although many students go directly to college after high school graduation, some delay enrolling and take a gap year. An average of forty thousand to sixty thousand students take a gap year annually, according to the Gap Year Association, a nonprofit organization that helps students find gap year opportunities. Jennifer Sullivan, the founder of Fast Forward College Counseling, says that students and parents are becoming more aware of the benefits of taking a gap year and the opportunities for students. "It's not an all-or-nothing now. You're not just going to college or you're going to work. There's a lot of in-between. There's a lot of gray area where some students do choose to take a gap year or to take a gap semester, then decide that they're ready,"[33] she says.

What Is a Gap Year?

A gap year is a semester or year typically taken after high school and before starting college or other education. Students often use a gap year to travel, work, or volunteer. Some students use the time away from the pressure of school to refresh and recharge. Others, who are unsure about what they want to study in college, use the time to think and plan their future.

The options are plentiful for students considering a gap year. Some organizations connect students with structured programs focusing on specific areas of interest. For example, the Gap Year Association lists programs focusing on ecology, animal welfare and conservation, language studies, coding, and more. Another organization, AmeriCorps, offers service programs for students ages eighteen and older. Students in an AmeriCorps program are eligible for a living allowance and an educational award that can pay off student loans or be used for future tuition.

Students can also create their own experiences during a gap year. They may decide to work to make money for college or take an internship to gain real-world experience or earn college credit. "The best gap years tend to be the ones that push students to think about who they are and their role in the world,"[34] says Joe O'Shea, dean of undergraduate studies at Florida State University.

For students who do not feel ready to jump into college, a gap year can give them the time to prepare. During the time away from school, they can pause and reflect on their interests and explore options before entering college. "Often you see students who

> "The best gap years tend to be the ones that push students to think about who they are and their role in the world."[34]
>
> —Joe O'Shea, dean of undergraduate studies at Florida State University

A gap year is time typically taken between high school and college. Usually, students use a gap year to travel, work, or volunteer. This time away from the pressure of school can refresh and recharge students.

struggle in higher education because they don't have a sense of purpose and direction," O'Shea says. "Gap years—because they give students a broader sense of the world and their place in it and how they can contribute—help to supply and empower students with the kind of motivation and purpose that can animate their entire college experience."[35]

Lexi, who decided to take a gap year after her 2020 high school graduation, says she was burned out from the stress of school:

> Trying to balance studying for APs [Advanced Placement tests], savoring the last months of high school with my friends, and now meeting college deadlines—I felt like I was under siege. I did not want to make important life decisions under that much stress. I wanted college to be something to look forward to, not another burden to bear as I struggle through my year. I felt constrained in the school system, bound not only by rules, habits and schedules, but also by relationships, expectations and responsibilities. I thought to myself, maybe it didn't have to be this hard. I wanted to escape, and so I did.[36]

Lexi embarked on a journey through Spain during her gap year. She says her solo travels challenged her and made her a

The Disadvantages of a Gap Year

Taking a gap year can have many benefits, but there are drawbacks as well. Students who take a year off can find it more challenging to return to school and regular study habits. They may also feel behind academically and socially because some of their classmates will already have a year of college experience. Gap years spent traveling, volunteering, and enjoying life experiences can also be expensive. They require careful planning so that these individuals do not waste time or the opportunities offered. And sometimes, taking a break from education can cause students to lose momentum, and they never return to school. When students forgo college entirely, they miss out on the career resources and networking colleges offer, putting them at a potential lifetime earnings disadvantage.

stronger person. "I became confident, independent, excited about life, comfortable in my body, secure in my relationship with myself, I felt calm and gentle and strong, as opposed to the small ball of anxiety that I had been at the end of my high school studies,"[37] she says.

Gap Year and College Admissions

If you are considering taking a gap year, you can still apply to college as a high school senior. It is usually easier to apply to college when you are still in high school because you can access teachers and counselors. You should also research the college you are interested in regarding its policy for gap years. However, most college admissions counselors recommend that students not reveal during the application process that they are considering taking a gap year.

Once a student is admitted, they can talk to an admissions officer about a gap year. Many colleges will want to know why the student is taking the gap year and may ask for paperwork. Some schools have policies for students taking a gap year, such as requiring them to check in midyear or not allowing students to take classes at another college. Colleges usually allow students to defer their enrollment by paying a deposit to hold their spot until after the gap year.

Some students choose to take a gap year because they were not admitted to a school they wanted to attend. Taking a gap year may allow students to gain experiences that may help them stand out when they reapply to the school. Some of the most successful gap year applicants show a connection between how they spent their gap year and their academic and future goals. "Not every gap year is created equally or is seen by admissions officers as credible. What you're looking for is, what did they do during that gap year to actually grow their academic profile?"[38] says Colleen Paparella, founder of DC College Counseling.

Is a Gap Year Right for You?

If you are considering a gap year, you should plan for what that time away from school will look like. You may plan to work, travel, or recharge, but you should have a specific reason for taking the gap year and a plan for how and when it will end. Some students decide against taking a gap year because they do not want to miss out on the academic and social opportunities and experiences that their friends still in school will have.

Finances are also a consideration when deciding whether to take a gap year and what to do with it. Formal programs and international travel can be costly, even with scholarships and financial aid. However, some organizations have established programs to support gap year students and to help make the experiences affordable and available to students from various backgrounds.

Exploring Careers

Some students use a gap year to gain experience working in their chosen field. Internships can offer firsthand experiences at work in a particular industry or job. Some may be paid, but many are unpaid. Syracuse University student Noa Putman decided to take a gap year between her freshman and sophomore years at the university. Her school had moved most classes online due to the 2020 COVID-19 pandemic, and Putman felt online learning was not as effective for her. Instead, she spent the year working in several jobs and internships.

Putman interned for *Everyday Health* magazine as an associate video producer during her gap year. She also worked as a production assistant for a documentary, assisted with photos for an interior designer, and worked on several other video projects. She felt that her experiences during the gap year allowed her to take a break from academic classes but still learn skills that would be helpful in her future career. "It was learning in a different way," she says. "Taking a year off honestly made me more excited to come back and gave me a little bit more direction going forward

Some students use a gap year to gain experience working as an intern in their chosen field. This can help them gain a better understanding of what their strengths and interests are.

about what I wanted to study and being more appreciative of even some of my classes that were in my major."[39]

The gap year experience also allowed Putman to earn money and rent an apartment for the first time. She was able to develop life skills, such as budgeting, saving, and paying bills, which she can use in the future. "It did teach me about finances in a way that I never really was forced to learn a little bit earlier,"[40] she says.

Putman admits that returning to school after the gap year was a bit of an adjustment. Yet she was ultimately able to fall back into her college routine. The gap year was beneficial for her, and she is glad she did it. However, Putman recognizes that taking a gap year might not work for everyone. "All I know is that I do think that I made

> "It was learning in a different way. Taking a year off honestly made me more excited to come back and gave me a little bit more direction going forward about what I wanted to study."[39]
>
> —Noa Putman, a student who worked during her gap year

the right call for myself, but I do think that everybody has their own timing and pace when it comes to school. It's an individual choice for sure, but I'm very happy with the one I made,"[41] she says.

Travel the World

Many students use a gap year to explore the world outside their home country. Some students travel to learn about new cultures, whereas others focus on studying new languages. Gap year travel programs can be structured, or you can create your own itinerary. Although traveling can quickly become expensive, gap year students can often save money by landing scholarships, working while abroad, or joining a volunteer program that pays for room and board.

Daisy Shepherd traveled to India and Laos during her gap year after graduating from high school in Seattle. She traveled around northern India for four months with nine students and two educators as part of a gap year program. "We stayed with local communities getting to know people and exploring places that tourists don't generally visit. We also volunteered in each place, including working with Tibetan refugees in Dharamshala and disabled children in Kolkata,"[42] says Shepherd. After India, Shepherd spent five months in Laos through another gap year

A Mental Health Break

Sometimes, a gap year can be a time to reset mental health. Brian Thompson felt lost at the end of his sophomore year at Syracuse University. He was unsure about his future and struggled with his mental health. He decided to take a gap year and use the time off to reset. Thompson spent his gap year working and attending therapy for his mental health. He says that the gap year helped him mature and get into a better frame of mind about school and his future. Without that time off, Thompson says he is unsure whether he would have been able to return to college. "It doesn't have to be a whole year, but I would recommend anyone to take the time off if they feel like they're kind of struggling," he says.

Quoted in Betsy Hart, "SU Students Share Gap Year Experiences and Benefits," The NewsHouse, February 4, 2022. www.thenewshouse.com.

AmeriCorps volunteers make benches in New York City. Many American students use their gap year to volunteer or perform service work in the United States or abroad.

program, where she taught five English classes, including one focused on sewing.

Shepherd explains that traveling and interacting with people from different countries and cultures has helped her feel more connected to people worldwide. "I've gained that feeling of being part of a global community. When we hear things are happening in faraway places, we're both connected and disconnected because we hear them through a media lens. Once you've put yourself in a place—you've put your body there and met the people there—it's hard to feel desensitized,"[43] she says.

Volunteer Your Time

Many American students use their gap year to volunteer or perform service work in the United States or abroad. There are many volunteer opportunities for students in education, health, conservation, and more. Some organizations will provide food and lodging for volunteers, while others, like AmeriCorps, will pay a small stipend.

One example of a service program for gap year students is the AmeriCorps City Year program. City Year recruits three thousand young people each year to serve full time in public schools

> "City Year is the motivation and focus you need after high school to find out which field you're passionate about, whether you want to go to college or take an alternate path."[45]
>
> —Claire Dempsey, a student who spent a gap year volunteering

in high-poverty areas as student success coaches. The volunteers work as tutors, mentors, and role models to help students build their social, emotional, and academic skills. Often, they can make a significant difference in a student's life. "City Year continues to be a powerful part of our school programming. [Volunteers] develop strong professional relationships with the students and for some students they are the reason that the students come to school,"[44] said one school principal in a 2021 survey.

After high school graduation, Claire Dempsey spent a gap year in a New York City school as a City Year volunteer. "Service and giving back to the community are a big part of how I was raised," she says. Dempsey found the work emotional and frustrating at times but also incredibly rewarding, as she explains:

> It's different than traveling or doing part-time work. City Year is full-time, and you will work harder than you ever have before. You will also mature, gain valuable skills and meet some of the most compassionate teammates who will become your lifelong best friends, all while devoting yourself to a cause greater than self. City Year is the motivation and focus you need after high school to find out which field you're passionate about, whether you want to go to college or take an alternate path.[45]

Gap year programs and activities are, as Dempsey maintains, a chance to mature and gain skills that can help move you forward on your path to a rewarding career. Having that time before going to college or a vocational school or pursuing another option provides valuable opportunities to become motivated and focused on your future.

CHAPTER FIVE

Alternatives to College

College is not for everyone. Some teens are not ready, and others do not want to go into debt for a degree. Fortunately, there are more options after high school than college. And many of those options can lead to secure, well-paying careers.

Apprenticeships

Apprenticeships are one path to a successful career. An apprenticeship trains people in the skills they need for a particular trade or profession. Most apprenticeship programs include both classroom learning and hands-on work experience. Today most apprenticeship programs last about three to four years, although some may be as short as twelve months.

Apprenticeships are common in skilled trades, such as carpentry, electrical wiring and repair, transportation, manufacturing, and plumbing. They are also becoming more popular in professional industries such as information technology, health care, business, and finance. Each apprenticeship program has specific requirements. Many demand that applicants be at least sixteen years old, but some want apprentices to be at least eighteen. Many also require apprentices to have a high school diploma or general equivalency diploma.

One benefit of an apprenticeship is getting paid while also receiving on-the-job training. "You are an employee, and you are learning on the job while you are learning in the classroom as well. So, not only are you making enough money to get by, but you're also getting that experience that most people have to wait for until they graduate with their degree to obtain,"[46] says Matt Devereaux, an apprenticeship success coordinator at West Michigan Works! Many apprenticeships pay higher-than-average salaries. According to Apprenticeship.gov, 92 percent of apprentices who complete their programs keep their jobs and earn an average annual salary of $72,000. The average person with a high school diploma makes a little more than $40,000 according to the Bureau of Labor Statistics. Apprentices also have access to health insurance and other benefits through their employers.

Apprentices learn from a mentor who is a professional in the field. Upon completion of an apprenticeship, participants earn a nationally recognized certificate. This certificate shows employers that the student has the skills necessary for a job. Some apprenticeship programs can count as college credits.

For young people unsure about what they want to do, apprenticeships can be a way to explore specific career fields without going into debt. "College is an extremely expensive career exploration activity, both emotionally and financially. Giving young people the opportunity to try, explore, and prepare for occupations through apprenticeships, opens their horizons, it does not tighten them,"[47] says Andrea Messing-Mathie, director at Jobs for the Future's Center for Apprenticeship and Work-Based Learning. Still, Messing-Mathie emphasizes that choosing an apprenticeship does not close the door to college. Many people finish an apprenticeship program and later earn a four-year college degree.

> "Giving young people the opportunity to try, explore, and prepare for occupations through apprenticeships, opens their horizons, it does not tighten them."[47]
>
> —Andrea Messing-Mathie, director at Jobs for the Future's Center for Apprenticeship and Work-Based Learning

Apprenticeships are becoming more popular in professional industries such as information technology. One benefit of an apprenticeship is getting paid while also receiving on-the-job training.

Some employers encourage their employees to attend college by offering to pay for some or all educational expenses.

David Swan, a twenty-six-year-old father of two, joined an apprenticeship program with Lee's Air in Fresno, California, in 2019. The program trains skilled workers in heating, ventilation, and air-conditioning (HVAC). Tom Howard, the owner of Lee's Air, says the apprenticeship program is a tool to address a growing labor shortage in his industry. "The reality is, as air conditioning and plumbing companies, we are desperate for labor. It's a massive problem,"[48] says Howard. Lee's Air pays for training and supplies and offers its apprentices full-time jobs at the company. Once workers finish the program, they often stay with the company. Swan still works for Lee's Air as a skilled HVAC technician. Someday, he might return to school to pursue a college degree in architecture, but for now, he feels he is in a promising career.

Joining the Military

For those who do not want to go to college right after high school, joining the military is another way to jump-start a career. Service members receive specialized training in many fields and learn valuable skills. They also earn a paycheck and have access to health care and other benefits for themselves and their families. Service members often can travel for overseas assignments and have access to educational benefits if they later decide to pursue a college degree.

To join the military, you must meet specific minimum requirements, including being at least seventeen years old (with parental consent) and being a US citizen. Potential service members must also pass fitness and health tests.

If you join the military, you will receive technical training, which allows you to earn certificates, licenses, and other credentials in

Army and air force technicians prepare for a training exercise. If you join the military, you will receive technical training that you can use for civilian jobs. In addition, serving in the military will also help you improve teamwork and leadership skills.

a specific field that you can use for civilian jobs. In addition, serving in the military will also help you improve teamwork and leadership skills and provide more hands-on experience than you will get in a classroom. Some service members choose to stay in the military for their entire careers. Others get work experience and learn skills in the military that they use in civilian jobs after their service is completed.

> "If you know someone who's feeling incredibly lost and they're particularly young, recommend them to the military."[49]
>
> —Jordan Mendiola, a young man who joined the army after high school

As a high school senior, Jordan Mendiola was unsure if college was right for him. He committed to attending Washington State University but then changed his mind. Instead, he joined the army. "I didn't know what I wanted to do with my life, so I joined. It was a big risk that came with having to potentially deploy and leave everything behind, but I felt like I had nothing to lose, so the upside outweighed the downside," says Mendiola. In the army, Mendiola worked as a construction engineer. He says that his time in the military helped him focus on what he wanted to do with his life. Today, he works in finance for a large bank and does freelance writing and blogging. Mendiola comments,

> If you know someone who's feeling incredibly lost and they're particularly young, recommend them to the military. It's a highly rewarding career path that has helped me find myself and do the things I want in life. It was the mental reset I needed after high school in order to start a new journey. There's nothing I would change about my decision to join the Army after high school. If I could go back in time, I'd do it all over again.[49]

Become a Digital Nomad

Are you interested in traveling the world? Digital nomads make a living while traveling to different parts of the United States and

Become an Entrepreneur

Did you know that Facebook founder Mark Zuckerberg never finished college? And he is not alone among entrepreneurs. According to a CNBC survey, less than half of small business owners have a college degree. Although a college education can be helpful when running a business, many of the skills you will need as an entrepreneur can be learned through real-world work experience, including communication, time management, and problem-solving skills. Other skills, such as financial management, marketing, and negotiation, can be learned through online courses or certificate programs. Although a college degree is not necessary to be an entrepreneur, you still must learn to know your business and market to help your company thrive. You might also benefit from small business programs (often run through community centers or local colleges) that help entrepreneurs acquire business loans, test market products, and connect with industry leaders who can provide valuable advice.

abroad. With a laptop and an internet connection, you can work almost anywhere. Some popular digital nomad jobs that do not require a college degree include writer or blogger, photographer, digital assistant, house sitter, and English teacher.

Depending on where you travel, many countries have a lower cost of living than the United States. In these places, digital nomads can support themselves with less money. And because digital nomads can help countries encourage travel and tourism, they may offer digital nomads some advantages, such as waiving taxes in return for staying in the country for a period.

To be successful as a digital nomad, you will need to be skilled in areas such as writing or photography. But you do not need to go to college to learn these skills, and often you can take online or in-person classes or even learn through hands-on experience. For example, photography can be a promising career for digital nomads. You can take pictures of the areas where you travel or stay for a time. You can sell the photos privately, put them in galleries, or market them to publishers.

Living and working as a digital nomad and seeing the world sounds enticing. However, there are some drawbacks that you should be aware of before you embark on this career path. A digital nomad lifestyle can be unpredictable and does not have the stability of a steady paycheck. What if your laptop has a problem or you cannot get an internet connection? Digital nomad jobs rarely come with benefits such as health insurance or retirement plans, so you must get these on your own. To be successful, you will have to have a lot of self-discipline to pull yourself away from the beach or adventure to get work done, or else you will not be paid. And traveling around the world by yourself can become lonely if you go months without seeing family and friends back home. "When I first set out on my digital nomad journey, I didn't have a clear view of my goals. All I wanted was to travel and to write. Those are perfectly respectable and reasonable desires, but without clear, specific goals and a concrete plan on how to achieve them, I was left feeling overwhelmed and aimless and my productivity suffered,"[50] says Kimberli, who works as a digital nomad from locations worldwide.

Living and working as a digital nomad and seeing the world sounds enticing. However, there are some drawbacks that you should be aware of before you embark on this career path.

Getting a Job

After high school graduation, some students may want a break before heading off for more full-time education. Others are tired of school and never really enjoyed it at all. And for some people, working after high school instead of enrolling in college is a financial decision. These students may decide to get an entry-level job.

There are several benefits to working after high school. First, you will be able to earn money instead of spending it on college tuition. Taking a year or two off from school to work and to save money can help pay for educational costs in the future and minimize the amount of debt you will incur to pay for it. Taking a year or more away from school can also give students the time and perspective to better appreciate a college education. They may also better understand what fields they are interested in and explore different options.

While working, you will likely be exposed to a wider variety of people than you were in high school. You will meet and interact with people with diverse personalities and backgrounds. You will also gain independence and learn how to manage and budget your paycheck. Living independently will give you more life experience, including paying rent and utilities as well as buying groceries, gas, and more.

If you choose to work after high school, you can learn valuable skills and move up the career ladder in a company or field. Some

Build a Freelance Portfolio

Whether you plan to travel the world as a digital nomad or just want to work on your own terms as a freelancer, building a portfolio can help showcase your work to potential clients and help you land the jobs you want. Whether your skills are writing, photography, website development, or something else, a portfolio is your most important marketing tool. A portfolio is a collection of your best work, and it highlights your skills and abilities. It should display your range of skills and any specialties you offer. A portfolio should be well organized and easy for potential clients to view and understand. It should also be updated frequently to showcase your latest work to help you land the jobs you want.

companies offer specialized training and value work experience more than a college degree. However, you can still go to college if you change your mind.

In recent years, a tight labor market has driven a growing number of companies, including Google, Tesla, and IBM, to drop requirements for employees to have a bachelor's degree for specific jobs, according to a 2022 study by researchers at *Harvard Business Review* and Emsi Burning Glass, a leading labor market data company. Instead, these companies are focusing more on skills-based hiring to find the right employees for the jobs. "A person's educational credentials are not the only indicators of success, so we advanced our approach to hiring to focus on skills, experiences and potential,"[51] says Jimmy Etheredge, CEO of Accenture North America.

Bank of America has changed its hiring practices to focus more on skills than degrees. "We recognize that prospective talent think they need a degree to work for us, but that is not the case. We are dedicated to recruiting from a diverse talent pool to provide an equal opportunity for all to find careers in financial services, including those that don't require a degree,"[52] says Christie Gragnani-Woods, an executive with Bank of America Global Talent Acquisition.

> "A person's educational credentials are not the only indicators of success, so we advanced our approach to hiring to focus on skills, experiences and potential."[51]
>
> —Jimmy Etheredge, CEO of Accenture North America

Many Options

After high school, students have many options to pursue a career. For some students, enrolling in college and earning a four-year degree is an excellent path to a well-paying job. However, traditional college is not the only path to a satisfying career. Students can learn the skills they need to succeed in various ways, from community college and online school to vocational schools and work experience. And you are not stuck with what you pick right out of high school. Many students change their minds about college or careers and go back to school or find their fit on a different educational path.

SOURCE NOTES

Introduction: An Important Decision

1. Quoted in Rebecca Koenig, "Guiding Young People Not to College or Careers—but to Good Lives," EdSurge, March 22, 2022. www.edsurge.com.
2. Quoted in Jessica Dickler, "College Is Still Worth It, Research Finds—Although Students Are Growing Skeptical," CNBC, March 1, 2023. www.cnbc.com.
3. Quoted in Koenig, "Guiding Young People Not to College or Careers."
4. Quoted in Koenig, "Guiding Young People Not to College or Careers."
5. Quoted in Koenig, "Guiding Young People Not to College or Careers."
6. Quoted in Associated Press, "Jaded with Education, More Americans Are Skipping College," Education Week, March 14, 2023. www.edweek.org.

Chapter One: Is College Right for You?

7. Quoted in Isaiah Atkins, "Can Your Alma Mater Help You Land a Job?," Business News Daily, February 21, 2023. www.businessnewsdaily.com.
8. Quoted in Danielle Gagnon, "Top 7 Reasons College Is Important," Southern New Hampshire University, September 19, 2022. www.snhu.edu.
9. Quoted in Daniel De Vise, "Twenty High-Paying Jobs That Don't Require a College Degree," *The Hill,* February 18, 2023. https://thehill.com.
10. Quoted in Jon Marcus, "High-Paying Jobs That Don't Need a College Degree? Thousands of Them Sit Empty," NPR, February 14, 2023. www.npr.org.
11. Quoted in Emma Kerr, "How Your College Choice Can Affect Job Prospects," *U.S. News & World Report,* December 16, 2020. www.usnews.com.
12. Quoted in Miranda Marquit, "Should I Go to College? 5 Signs a 4-Year School Isn't for You," LendingTree, November 16, 2020. www.lendingtree.com.
13. Quoted in Kenadi Silcox, "Why It's So Hard for College Students Who Are Parents to Actually Earn Their Degrees," *Money,* May 13, 2022. https://money.com.
14. Quoted in TheBestSchools.org, "Why You Should Go to Online College," August 17, 2022. https://thebestschools.org.
15. Quoted in Marquit, "Should I Go to College?"
16. Quoted in Marquit, "Should I Go to College?"

Chapter Two: How Will You Pay for College?

17. Quoted in Christy Rakoczy, Rebecca Safier, and Sage Evans, "Experts Reveal 18 Places to Find Scholarship Money for College," LendingTree, February 16, 2021. www.lendingtree.com.
18. Quoted in Rakoczy, Safier, and Evans, "Experts Reveal 18 Places to Find Scholarship Money for College."
19. Quoted in Kelly Burch, "I Paid for College Entirely with Scholarships and Grants. Here's What I Want Other Students and Parents to Know," Insider, December 15, 2022. www.insider.com.
20. Quoted in Burch, "I Paid for College Entirely with Scholarships and Grants."
21. Quoted in Burch, "I Paid for College Entirely with Scholarships and Grants."
22. Quoted in Emma Kerr, "Weighing the Pros and Cons of Working While in College," *U.S. News & World Report,* December 30, 2020. www.usnews.com.
23. Quoted in Jessica Dickler, "Many Companies Are Offering Generous Tuition Assistance So Workers Can Go Back to College," CNBC, September 2, 2021. www.cnbc.com.
24. Quoted in Dee-Ann Durbin and Anne D'Innocenzio, "Companies Like Starbucks and Chipotle Are Paying Hourly Employees' College Tuition. One Graduate Keeps Asking, 'Is This Real?,'" *Fortune,* October 23, 2022. https://fortune.com.
25. Quoted in Durbin and D'Innocenzio, "Companies Like Starbucks and Chipotle Are Paying Hourly Employees' College Tuition."

Chapter Three: Other Education Options

26. Quoted in Victor Valley College, "Respiratory Therapy: Success Stories." www.vvc.edu.
27. Quoted in Susan D'Agustino, "A Surge in Young Undergrads, Fully Online," Inside Higher Ed, October 14, 2022. www.insidehighered.com.
28. Quoted in D'Agustino, "A Surge in Young Undergrads, Fully Online."
29. Quoted in D'Agustino, "A Surge in Young Undergrads, Fully Online."
30. Quoted in Samantha York, "Trade Schools Take Hands-On Approach to Build Workforce Amid Higher Enrollment," CBS 21, October 18, 2022. https://local21news.com.
31. Quoted in Jon Marcus, "Long Disparaged, Education for the Skilled Trades Is Slowly Coming into Fashion," Hechinger Report, December 31, 2021. https://hechingerreport.org.
32. Quoted in *HyperionDev* (blog), "Student Success Story—Sean Van Loggerenberg—from Bartender to Web Developer," December 3, 2019. https://blog.hyperiondev.com.

Chapter Four: Taking a Gap Year

33. Quoted in Cole Claybourn, "How a Gap Year Prepares Students for College," *U.S. News & World Report,* November 29, 2022. www.usnews.com.
34. Quoted in Claybourn, "How a Gap Year Prepares Students for College."

35. Quoted in Claybourn, "How a Gap Year Prepares Students for College."
36. Quoted in Leaf Academy, "What Does It Take to Take a Gap Year? (Real Story by Lexi)," December 1, 2020. www.leafacademy.eu.
37. Quoted in Leaf Academy, "What Does It Take to Take a Gap Year?"
38. Quoted in Claybourn, "How a Gap Year Prepares Students for College."
39. Quoted in Betsy Hart, "SU Students Share Gap Year Experiences and Benefits," The NewsHouse, February 4, 2022. www.thenewshouse.com.
40. Quoted in Hart, "SU Students Share Gap Year Experiences and Benefits."
41. Quoted in Hart, "SU Students Share Gap Year Experiences and Benefits."
42. Quoted in *Your Teen Magazine,* "My Gap Year Story: I Got to Travel the World," June 12, 2019. https://yourteenmag.com.
43. Quoted in *Your Teen Magazine,* "My Gap Year Story: I Got to Travel the World."
44. Quoted in Kellie Hinkle, "Feedback from Key Partners: Teachers and Principals," City Year, August 25, 2021. www.cityyear.org.
45. Claire Dempsey, "A City Year Is More than Just a Gap Year," City Year, May 5, 2021. www.cityyear.org.

Chapter Five: Alternatives to College

46. Quoted in Heidi Rivera, "7 Reasons to Consider an Apprenticeship Before Going to College," MoneyUnder30, March 7, 2022. www.moneyunder30.com.
47. Quoted in Rivera, "7 Reasons to Consider an Apprenticeship Before Going to College."
48. Quoted in Jessica Dickler, "Apprenticeship Programs Are Becoming an Alternative to College," CNBC, February 15, 2023. www.cnbc.com.
49. Jordan Mendiola, "Joining the Army After High School Was a Good Decision," Medium, January 30, 2021. https://medium.com.
50. Kimberli, "How My Part-Time Passion Became a Full-Time Digital Nomad Lifestyle," Worldpackers, March 16, 2023. www.worldpackers.com.
51. Quoted in Susan Caminiti, "No College Degree? No Problem. More Companies Are Eliminating Requirements to Attract the Workers They Need," CNBC, April 25, 2022. www.cnbc.com.
52. Quoted in Lucas Mearian, "Companies Move to Drop College Degree Requirements for New Hires, Focus on Skills," *ComputerWorld*, August 10, 2022. www.computerworld.com.

GLOSSARY

apprenticeship: A program in which a person works to learn a trade.

certificate: A document that shows a person has completed a training program and learned specific skills.

digital nomad: A person who makes a living online while traveling the world.

financial aid: Money that is given or lent to students to pay for education.

fixed-rate loan: A loan with an interest rate that stays the same for the life of the loan.

gap year: A semester or year typically taken between high school and college in which a person travels, works, volunteers, or participates in another activity.

interest: The fee borrowers pay to lenders for borrowing money.

loan: Money borrowed from a bank or other financial institution.

Pell Grant: A federal grant available to students to pay for tuition.

scholarship: A form of financial aid that does not need to be repaid.

stipend: A fixed financial allowance usually provided to offset living expenses.

trade school: A school that prepares students for skilled jobs.

vocational training: Knowledge and skills that prepare a person for a particular job.

FOR MORE INFORMATION

Books

Tammy Gagne, *Paying for College*. San Diego: ReferencePoint, 2020.

Kevin Hayes, *Financial Literacy Information for Teens*. Detroit: Omnigraphics, 2021.

Genevieve Morgan, *Undecided: Navigating Life and Learning After High School*. Minneapolis: Zest, 2020.

Don Nardo, *Planning for College*. San Diego: ReferencePoint, 2020.

Virginia Vitzthum, *Money Matters for Teens: Advice on Spending and Saving, Managing Income, and Paying for College*. New York: Sky Pony, 2022.

Internet Sources

Justin Berkman, "Should You Go to College? 4 Pros and 3 Cons," *SAT/ACT Online Prep Blog*, PrepScholar, May 23, 2022. https://blog.prepscholar.com.

Daniel De Vise, "Twenty High-Paying Jobs That Don't Require a College Degree," *The Hill*, February 18, 2023. https://thehill.com.

Mark Kantrowitz, "How to Pay for College," Saving for College, November 10, 2022. www.savingforcollege.com.

Christy Rakoczy, Rebecca Safier, and Sage Evans, "Experts Reveal 18 Places to Find Scholarship Money for College," LendingTree, February 16, 2021. www.lendingtree.com.

Websites

College Board
www.collegeboard.org
The College Board is an American nonprofit organization that was formed to expand access to higher education. Its website has a career quiz and information about colleges and scholarships.

Explore the Trades

www.explorethetrades.org

Explore the Trades is an organization that aims to recruit people to careers in the trades. Its website has information about career opportunities and apprenticeships.

Federal Student Aid

https://studentaid.gov

Federal Student Aid, a part of the US Department of Education, is the largest provider of student financial aid in the nation. Its website has a link to the FAFSA form and information about student aid and loans.

Princeton Review

www.princetonreview.com

The Princeton Review is an educational services company providing tutoring, test preparation, and admissions resources for students. Its website has information about colleges, majors, and careers.

Scholarships.com

www.scholarships.com

Scholarships.com is a website students can use to search for scholarships by categories such as grade point average, military affiliation, ethnicity, and more.

INDEX

Note: Boldface page numbers indicate illustrations.

AmeriCorps, 37
  City Year program, 43–44
  volunteers in, **43**
apprenticeships, 45–47
  definition of, 57
Arnett, Jeffrey, 12
associate's degree, 27–29
  types of, 29
Association of Public and Land Grant Universities, 8

Bank of America, 53
Barlas, Christina, 30–31
Batista, Angela, 26
Bureau of Labor Statistics, 7, 35

Campbell, Samantha, 15
careers/occupations
  available to digital nomads, 50
  not requiring college degrees, 9–11
  requiring college degrees, 9
  requiring vocational skills, 32
  skills-based, 33, 34
Caruso, Krista, 29
Ceballos, Princesa, 4
Center on Education and the Workforce (Georgetown University), 10, 23
certificates/certificate programs, 33–35
  definition of, 57
Cheneau, Vernell, III, 5–6
Chipotle, 25–26
coding languages, 35
college
  academic preparation for, 15
  benefits of, 8–9
  careers requiring, 9
  cost of, 12, 17–18
  exposure to new subjects in, 11
  taking gap year before starting, 36–38
  See also factors in choosing college
college admissions, 18
  gap years and, 39
College Board, 33, 58
College of William and Mary, 12
community colleges, 13, 22
  degrees offered by, 28, 29
  transfer of credits from, 15

degree programs, percentage of college students not completing, 15
Dempsey, Claire, 44
digital nomads, 49–51
  definition of, 57

earnings/salary
  anticipated, student loan debt and, 22

for apprenticeships versus high school graduates, 46
    for college versus high school graduates, 8
ECMC Group, 5
Education Data Initiative, 15
employers
    dropping college degree requirements, 53
    tuition assistance programs offered by, 24–26
Emsi Burning Glass (labor market data company), 53
Etheredge, Jimmy, 53
Explore the Trades, 59

factors in choosing college
    academic preparation and, 15
    career goals as, 9–11
    financial, 12–13
    life circumstances as, 14–15
Farrell, Ryan, 10–11
Federal Student Aid, 59
financial aid, 12–13
    definition of, 57
    federal, free application for, 18, 21
    grants/scholarships, 18–21
    job earnings and, 24
    student loans, 21–22
Fisher, Dan, 5
fixed-rate loans, 21
    definition of, 57
Forbes (magazine), 33
Free Application for Federal Student Aid (FAFSA), 18, 21
freelance work, 49
    building portfolio for, 52
    as web developer, 35

Gap Year Association, 36
gap years, 36–37
    college admissions and, 39
    definition of, 57
    disadvantages to, 38
    exploring careers during, 40–42
    as mental health break, 42
    planning for, 40
    travel during, 42–43
    volunteering during, 43–44
Garcia, Luis, 33
Georgetown University, 10, 23
Google, 53
Gragnani-Woods, Christie, 53
grants/grant programs, 12, 18–19
Guild Education, 25

Harvard Business Review, 53
high school/high school graduates
    earnings for, 8, 46
    getting job after graduating, 52–53
    health/happiness among, 12
    taking gap year after, 36–38
    unemployment among, 8–9
Holcomb, Eric, 32

IBM, 53
income share agreement (ISA), 25
interest
    definition of, 57
    on Direct PLUS Loans, 22
    on federal student loans, 21

Jilek, Lydia, 24

Leach, Samantha, 19–20

LeBlanc, Paul, 30
loans
   definition of, 57
   See also student loans

Malave, Danielle, 26
Margie, Andrew, 9
marketable skills, developing, 16
McQueen, Ken, 29
Meuse, Victoria, 9
military, 48–49
Morgan, Garret, 11

National Student Clearinghouse, 6
Next Level Jobs initiative (Indiana), 32

on-the-job training, 29
opinion polls. *See* surveys
O'Shea, Joe, 37–38

Paparella, Colleen, 39
Pell Grants, 18
   definition of, 57
polls. *See* surveys
portfolios, building freelance, 52
Princeton Review, 59
private loans, 22
Pulsipher, Scott, 30
Putman, Noa, 40–41

remote learning/online college programs, 15
Rose, Tysa, 14–15

salary. *See* earnings/salary
Santos, Jose, 33
Scholarships.com, 59

scholarships/scholarship programs, 12, 18, 19–20
   definition of, 57
Shepherd, Daisy, 42
skills
   assessing, in determining career goals, 9
   associate's degree and, 27, 29
   certificate programs and, 33–34
   developing marketable, 16, 35
   hiring based on, 53
   learned from work after high school, 16
   vocational programs and, 32
Smith, Mack, 13, 16
Starbucks, 25
Stezala, Kim, 18
stipends, 24, 26, 43
   definition of, 57
Stokes, Jamia, 7
student loans, 12–13, 21–22
   income share agreements and, 25
Sullivan, Jennifer, 36
surveys
   on college degrees among business owners, 50
   of high school student on plans to attend fully online colleges, 30

technical schools, 10
Tesla, 53
Thompson, Brian, 42
trade schools, 32
   definition of, 57
travel
   as digital nomad, 50–51
   during gap year, 42–43

tuition assistance programs, 24–26

undergraduate enrollment, decline in, 6–7
unemployment, among college versus high school graduates, 8–9
U.S. News & World Report (magazine), 12

Van Der Werf, Martin, 11
Van Loggerenberg, Sean, 35

Vasconcelos, Shannon, 23
vocational programs/training, 32–33
definition of, 57
volunteers/volunteering
AmeriCorps, **43**
during gap year, 36, 38, 42, 43–44

Walmart, 25
web developer, 35

Zuckerberg, Mark, 50

PICTURE CREDITS

Cover: Monkey Business Images/Shutterstock

6: 4 PM production/Shutterstock
10: Rawpixel.com/Shutterstock
13: Drazen Zigic/Shutterstock
14: Funnyangel/Shutterstock
19: Leigh Trail/Shutterstock
20: Monkey Business Images/Shutterstock
23: Fizkes/Shutterstock
28: WESTOCK PRODUCTIONS/Shutterstock
31: Fizkes/Shutterstock
34: Wavebreakmedia/Shutterstock
37: Aslysun/Shutterstock
41: Gorodenkoff/Shutterstock
43: A katz/Shutterstock
47: Gorodenkoff/Shutterstock
48: Kara Carrier/US Air Force
51: AYA Images/Shutterstock